GET THE MEASURE

Units and measurements

Rob Colson

Acknowledgments and Picture credits

Published in paperback in Great Britain in 2019 by The Watts Publishing Group

Copyright © The Watts Publishing Group, 2017

Series editor: Sarah Peutrill

Produced by Tall Tree Ltd
Design: Ben Ruocco
Consultants: Hilary Koll and Steve Mills

ISBN: 978 1 4451 4952 3

Printed in China

MIX
Paper from responsible sources
FSC
www.fsc.org
FSC® C104740

Franklin Watts
An imprint of
Hachette Children's Group
Part of The Watts Publishing Group
Carmelite House
50 Victoria Embankment
London EC4Y 0DZ

An Hachette UK Company
www.hachette.co.uk

www.franklinwatts.co.uk

Picture credits:
t-top, b-bottom, l-left, r-right, c-centre, front cover-fc, back cover-bc
All images courtesy of Dreamstime.com, unless indicated:
Inside front Professor25; fc, bc Pablo631; fcbl Markbeckwith; fctc Radub85; 1c, 17t Supsup; 41 Gekaskr; 41 Ekaterina Nikolaenko; 4b Justk8; 5c Hjalmeida; 5cb Koszivu; 6c, 28tl Johan63; 7b, 16bc, 29tc Msanca; 8b, 30bl Mzwonko; 9 NASA; 9c, 17c Mexrix; fccb, 10l Hamster3d; 10c, 22br, 31tr Macrovector; bcc, 11t Tverdohlib; 11b NASA; 12t Frameangel; fcbl, 12c Experimental; 12b Mrallen; 13b Filipefrazao84; 15c NASA; 15b Blakeley; 16t Zaclurs; 16tr Roberto Giovannini; 16bl Dragon_27; 16bc Shaeree Mukherjee; 16br Bokicai; 17c Fallsview; 17bl, 29tr Insima; 17c Ciro Amedeo Orabona; 17br Red33; 18t Mrmarshall; 18b Nicolasprimola; fctl, 19t Rudall30; 19b Red Orbit; bctr, 20b Cory Thoman; fcbr, 21t, 29br Forplayday; fcbr, 21t, 29br Dundanim/shutterstock.com; 21b, 28tr NASA; bctc, 22t Zinchik; 23tr Leo Blanchette; 23bl Nicolas Fernandez; 23bc Dannyphoto80; 23bc Jehsomwang; 23br Topgeek; 24b Razvan Ionut Dragomirescu; 24t Vectorlibellule; 25c Pppfoto15; fctr, 25b Tuja66; 26l Onairjiw; 27t Roman Yatsyna; 27c Haiyin; 27b Rasà Messina Francesca; fctc, 28b drmakkoy/iStockphoto.com; 30tc Tuuljumala; 30br Milosluz; 32t Stylephotographs

Contents

A history of **measuring** 4

Length and **distance** 6

Huge distances 8

Tiny distances 10

Area 12

Volume 14

Speed and **velocity** 16

Weight and **mass** 18

Temperature 20

Telling the **time** 22

What are we **measuring?** 24

How **fast** is your **computer?** 26

Quiz 28

Glossary 31

Index and **Answers** 32

A history of measuring

When people first moved into towns and cities thousands of years ago, they needed systems of measurement. These allowed them to build homes, make clothes and tools and trade with one another.

1 cubit

The earliest known standard measurement is the cubit from ancient Egypt. It is based on the length from the end of the fingers to the elbow.

Rule of thumb

'Rule of thumb' is a phrase that means a rough estimate of a measurement. Carpenters used to use their thumbs rather than rulers to measure their work. In many languages, the word for the length 'inch' also means 'thumb'.

In some countries, horses are measured using hands. The height of a horse is measured from the ground to its withers. Thoroughbred horses used for racing are about 16 hands high.

Body measures

The imperial system of measurement was devised for the British Empire in the 19th century. It has many lengths based on parts of the body. A few countries still use imperial measurements, but most countries have switched to metric.

1 inch
about 2.5 cm. This is about the width of a thumb.

1 foot = 12 inches
about 30 cm. This is about the length of a foot.

1 hand = 4 inches
about 10 cm. This is about the width of a hand.

1 yard = 3 feet
about 90 cm. This is about the length of a stride.

Approx. 10 cm

Approx. 30 cm

Going metric

Today's standard international units of measurement, known as the metric system, were devised in revolutionary France over 200 years ago.

In the 18th century, there were thousands of different units of measurement, and each town or area had its own system. In 1791, following the Revolution, the French decided to create one standard for all, based on multiples of ten. The measures are all derived from the standard length of **1 metre** (see page 6), and include measures of weight and volume.

Length and distance

The metric unit of length is the metre. It was defined in 1793 by the French Academy of Sciences as one ten-millionth of the distance on Earth's surface from the equator to the North or South poles.

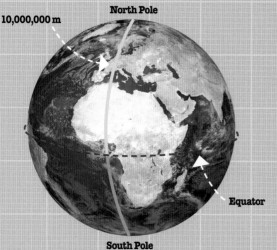

10,000,000 m
North Pole
Equator
South Pole

Today, the metre is defined exactly as the distance travelled by light in $1/299{,}792{,}458$ of a second.

Smaller distances start in millimetres, which can then be converted into centimetres and then metres.

1,000 mm = 100 cm = 1 m

Longer distances are often described in kilometres.

1 km = 1,000 m

Some countries still use the imperial measurement the mile to describe distances.

1 mile = 1.609344 km

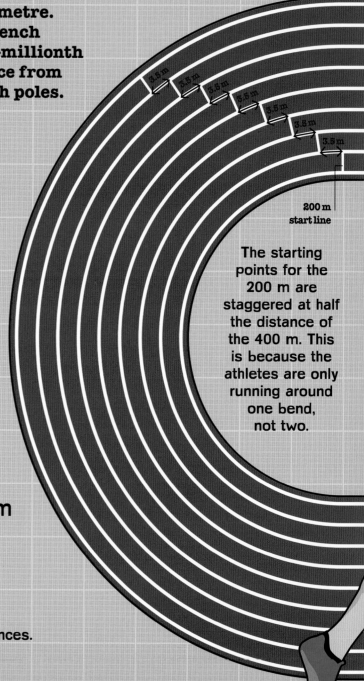

3.5 m
3.5 m
3.5 m
3.5 m
3.5 m
3.5 m
3.5 m

200 m start line

The starting points for the 200 m are staggered at half the distance of the 400 m. This is because the athletes are only running around one bend, not two.

Leagues

In the Middle Ages (5th–15th centuries), a common way to describe longer distances was the league. This was the distance a person could walk in an hour, which was roughly 5 kilometres, or 3 miles. People without horses would sometimes walk several days at a time to get from one town to another. If a town was 30 leagues away, you needed to allow 30 hours of walking to get there.

"I think I'll stick to the 100 metres next time!"

Ready, set, go

One lap of an athletics track is 400 m, but that's only if you run right on the inside. When athletes compete in a 400 m race, their starting points are staggered so that they all run the same distance. A full lap in the outside lane is about 450 m.

Inside lane

400 m start line

Start lane 1
Start lane 2
Start lane 3
Start lane 4
Start lane 5
Start lane 6
Start lane 7
Start lane 8

7m 7m 7m 7m 7m 7m 7m

FINISH

Huge distances

Kuiper belt

Sun

10

Neptune

100

The Sun is 150,000,000 kilometres from Earth. Astronomers call this distance 1 AU (Astronomical Unit). Here is the Solar System with distances from the Sun in AU.

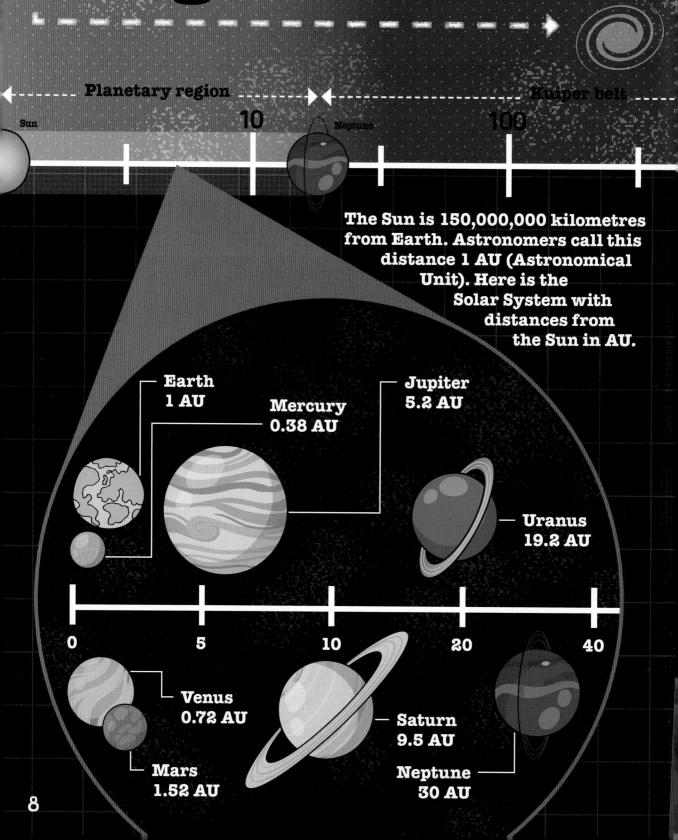

Earth
1 AU

Mercury
0.38 AU

Jupiter
5.2 AU

Uranus
19.2 AU

0 5 10 20 40

Venus
0.72 AU

Saturn
9.5 AU

Mars
1.52 AU

Neptune
30 AU

Oort cloud

1,000   10,000   100,000 AU

Light year

To measure the enormous distances between stars, astronomers use a unit called a light year. This is equal to the distance travelled in one year by light, the fastest thing in the Universe.

1 light year (ly) = 9.5 trillion kilometres.
That's **9,500,000,000,000 km**
1 ly = 60,000 AU

The nearest star to Earth after the Sun is Alpha Centauri. **It is 4.4 ly** away, meaning that it is 264,000 times farther away from us than the Sun.

Alpha Centauri

Andromeda Galaxy

MACS0647-JD

Our Solar System is part of the Milky Way galaxy. This is a disc of stars **1,000 ly thick** and **100,000 ly across**. The nearest galaxy to the Milky Way is **Andromeda**. It is **2.5 million ly** from Earth.

The farthest galaxy we have spotted is **MACS0647-JD** galaxy, which is **13.3 billion ly** away. That means that the light that we are seeing now left the galaxy 13.3 billion years ago. We are seeing MACS0647-JD as it was a very long time ago – before Earth even existed.

Tiny
distances

The smallest life forms, bacteria, are just a few microns across.

1 micron (μm) = 1 millionth of a metre

The molecules that code for life, **DNA**, are about 2 nanometres (nm) across. These molecules are made of long chains of smaller molecules that are tightly coiled up. If DNA molecules were stretched out straight, they would be several centimetres long.

1 nanometre (nm) = 1 billionth of a metre

A hydrogen atom is about 25 picometres (pm) across.

1 picometre (pm) = 1 trillionth of a metre

Beard-second

Not content with the standard measurements, physics students in the US invented a measurement of their own.

A beard-second is defined as the length a man's beard grows in one second. There is some dispute as to how far that really is, but it's normally taken to be 5 nm. That's

0.000000005 m

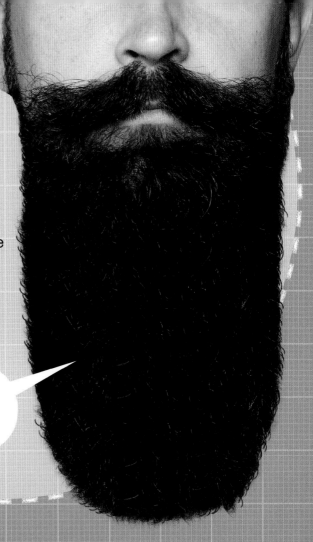

"Slow down, I'm growing faster than a beard-second!"

The shortest length possible

Physicists calculate that there is a minimum length that cannot be divided up. This is called the Planck length, and it is about

10^{-35} m – that's $1/10^{35}$ m.

The smallest thing we can see with the naked eye is a dot about 0.1 mm across: ⟶ If that dot were blown up to the size of the entire universe, a dot inside the dot that is 1 Planck length across would appear to be about **0.1 mm across**.

Nanotechnology

Nanotechnologists develop tiny machines out of individual molecules. They make motors, switches, gears and pumps just a few hundred nanometres across. These miniature machines could be used by doctors to deliver medicines around the body.

In 2011, scientists made the first-ever molecule-sized motor, just 1 nm across.

These highly magnified nanogears are made from carbon nanotubes with benzene molecules attached on the outside to form interlocking 'teeth'.

Area

Area is a measure of the amount of surface a two-dimensional shape covers. The basic metric unit of area is the square metre, m², which is the area of a square with sides one metre long.

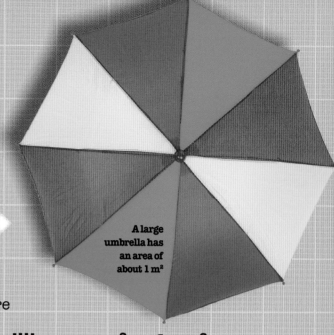

A large umbrella has an area of about 1 m²

Squaring a metre

There are 1,000 millimetres in a metre. This means that on each side of a square metre there are 1,000 millimetres, so there are **1,000 x 1,000 = 1 million mm²** in **1 m²**.

1 acre

1 hectare

Measuring land

In metric, land area is measured in hectares.

1 hectare = 10,000 m², and is a little larger than a football pitch.

A day's work

The imperial measurement of land area is the acre.

1 acre = 0.404 hectares.

The acre was fixed in medieval times as the amount of land that could be ploughed using a pair of oxen in one day.

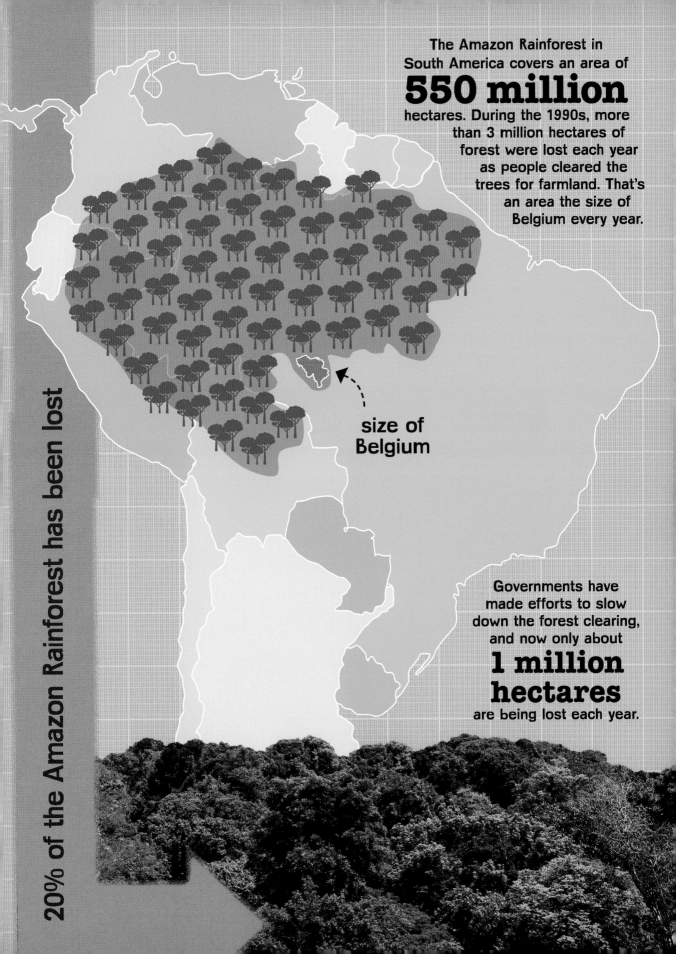

The Amazon Rainforest in South America covers an area of **550 million** hectares. During the 1990s, more than 3 million hectares of forest were lost each year as people cleared the trees for farmland. That's an area the size of Belgium every year.

size of Belgium

Governments have made efforts to slow down the forest clearing, and now only about **1 million hectares** are being lost each year.

20% of the Amazon Rainforest has been lost

Volume

1 m

1 m

1 m

1 m

Volume is the amount of space inside a three-dimensional object. The litre is the basic metric unit of volume.

A litre is the volume of a cube with 10 cm sides. It contains

10 x 10 x 10 = 1,000 cm³.

1 cm³

10 cm

There are 1,000 litres in 1 m³.

1 litre

1 foot

1 acre-foot

66 feet

660 feet

In the US, large quantities of water in reservoirs or rivers are measured using a unit called the acre-foot. This is the volume water that would cover an area of one acre to a depth of one foot.

1 acre-foot
= just over 1,233 cubic metres

Shipping volume

Freight is carried around the world in container ships. Container-size is measured using a unit called a **TEU**. TEU stands for

Twenty-foot Equivalent Unit

Containers that are 1 TEU big are

20 feet (6.1 metres) long.

Their ends are squares with 8 ft (2.4 m) sides. Containers are a standard size so that they can be stacked next to one another. Most containers are 40 ft (12.2 m) long, making them 2 TEU big. This is a good size to be pulled by a lorry once the container has been unloaded from the ship.

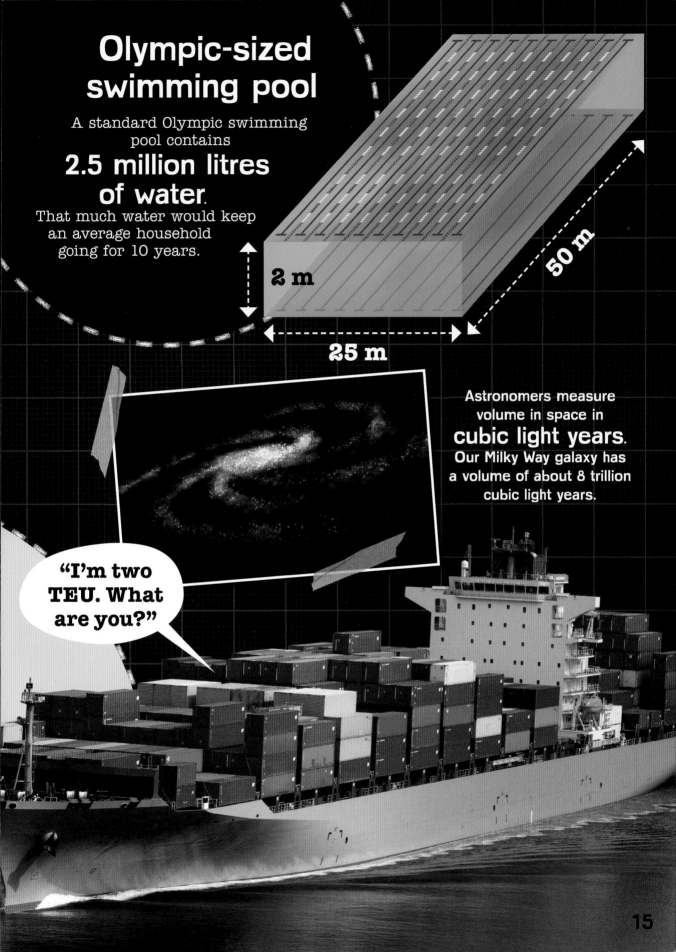

Olympic-sized swimming pool

A standard Olympic swimming pool contains
2.5 million litres of water.
That much water would keep an average household going for 10 years.

2 m

50 m

25 m

Astronomers measure volume in space in
cubic light years.
Our Milky Way galaxy has a volume of about 8 trillion cubic light years.

"I'm two TEU. What are you?"

Speed and velocity

Speed is a measure of the distance travelled per unit of time. It is commonly measured in metres per second (m/s) or kilometres per hour (km/h). An object's velocity is its speed in a particular direction.

The force of gravity causes objects to accelerate towards the centre of Earth. The rate of acceleration is

9.8 m/s²

Acceleration

A change in an object's velocity by a force is called **acceleration**.

A change in speed caused by acceleration is measured in **metres per second per second**, or **m/s²**.

In orbit
A satellite orbits at a constant speed, but it is also accelerating! The force of gravity affects its velocity by changing its direction to keep it in orbit.

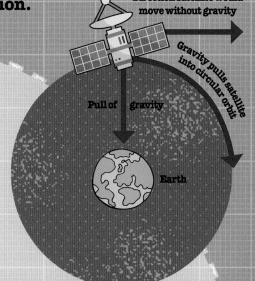

Direction satellite would move without gravity

Gravity pulls satellite into circular orbit

Pull of gravity

Earth

Earth's gravity constantly pulls the satellite to stop it from flying off. In much the same way, if you swing a yo-yo above your head, the string pulls it towards you.

Top speeds

Snail	Tortoise	Human	Race horse
1 m/h	8 km/h	45 km/h	70 km/h

Light speed

Light travels at **299,792,458** metres per second. Nothing can move faster than light speed, which physicist Albert Einstein (1879–1955) described as the speed limit of the Universe.

Thunder and lightning

The speed of sound through air is 340 m/s. The difference between the **speed of sound** and the **speed of light** is the reason we hear thunder after we see lightning. The light reaches us almost instantly but the sound may take many seconds. To work out how far away a lightning strike was, **count the seconds** between **seeing the lightning** and hearing the thunder. **Every three seconds represent one kilometre**.

Cheetah
100 km/h

Sail fish
110 km/h

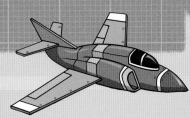

Fighter jet
3,500 km/h

Weight and mass

When we talk about how much something weighs, we are usually referring to its mass, which is a measure of how much matter the thing contains.

Weight is a measure of the **force of gravity** acting on an **object's mass**, pulling it towards the centre of Earth. We measure this force when we place an object on scales.

As the force of gravity is nearly the same everywhere on Earth, weighing an object tells us its mass.

The metric unit of measurement of mass is the kilogram (kg)

1 kg = 1,000 grams

1 gram is equal to the mass of 1 cubic centimetre of water.

The blue whale's tongue weighs as much as an elephant, while its heart weighs as much as a car.

Olympic weightlifting

Olympic weightlifters compete to raise weights above their heads. The weights are attached to a steel bar called a **barbell**. Equal weights, called **plates**, are attached at either end of the barbell, and secured in place with a **collar**. As the competition progresses, more and more weight is added. Weight increases by at least 1 kg at a time. The weights are as follows:

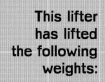

Barbell **20 kg**,
Collars (one at each end) **2.5 kg**
Plates: Large
Green **10 kg**
Yellow **15 kg**
Blue **20kg**
Red **25 kg**

Plates: Small
White **0.5 kg**
Green **1 kg**
Yellow **1.5 kg**
Blue **2 kg**
Red **2.5 kg**

This lifter has lifted the following weights:

Barbell (20 kg) + 2 x Collars (2 x 2.5 kg) + 2 x Large Red (2 x 25 kg) + 2 x Large Green (2 x 10 kg) + 2 x Small Yellow (2 x 1.5 kg)
= 98 kg

Weighing a tonne

One tonne equals 1,000 kg. The heaviest animal in the world, the blue whale, weighs **200 tonnes**. That's the weight of

2,500 adult humans.

The lightest mammal is the Etruscan shrew. It weighs just **1.8 grams**. One blue whale is equal to more than

100 million Etruscan shrews.

Etruscan shrew

Temperature

Temperature is measured using scales that are based on the freezing and boiling points of water. The most common scale used around the world is Celsius, but the Fahrenheit scale is also used. The boiling point of water is 100°C (212°F), while its freezing point is 0°C (32°F).

Converting

These are the formulas for converting between Celsius and Fahrenheit:

$$°F = (°C × \frac{9}{5}) + 32$$

$$°C = (°F - 32) × \frac{5}{9}$$

Absolute zero

An object's temperature is produced by the movement of atoms. The more rapidly the atoms move, the hotter the object becomes.

The temperature at which atoms would not move at all is known as **absolute zero**. This is a temperature of

−273.15°C

It is also defined as 0 Kelvin (0 K). 1 K equals absolute zero plus 1°C. Scientists believe that it is not possible to cool anything to 0 K, but they have managed to reach temperatures less than

1 billionth of a Kelvin.

Normal body temperature is between the range

36.1°C (96.7°F)

and 37.2°C (98.7°F).

If we become any colder or warmer, that means we are sick.

"Brrr...it's a bit nippy up here!"

The temperature in open space is a chilly 2.7 Kelvin. That's

-270.45°C

Moon temperatures

With no atmosphere to protect it, the temperature on the Moon drops to -150°C at night but soars to about 120°C during the day – literally boiling hot! Each time humans have landed on the Moon, the landing has been timed to happen just after the lunar dawn, before it has become too hot.

The temperature at the surface of the Sun is

5,500°C

At the Sun's core, it reaches more than 15 million °C.

Telling the time

We use a mix of measures to mark the passing of time, based on patterns our ancestors noticed in the changes of seasons, day and night.

A **year** is based on the time Earth takes to complete an orbit of the Sun, while a **day** is the time it takes for Earth to turn once completely on its axis.

Months are roughly equal to the time it takes the Moon to orbit Earth.

A sundial was an early clock that measured the time by showing the angle of the shadow of the Sun. It can only work during daytime.

Dividing the day

The ancient Greeks divided the daytime into 12 equal hours. As the amount of daylight varied through the year, the length of an hour varied — longer in summer and shorter in winter. The idea of dividing the whole day into 24 equal hours, also covering night-time, was first proposed by the Greek astronomer Hipparcus in the second century BCE, and this is the system we use today.

13.7 bya

The Universe starts with the Big Bang

13.4 bya

First galaxies start to form

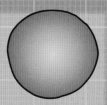

5 bya

The Sun forms

4.5 bya

Earth forms

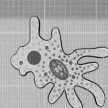

3.8 bya

First life forms appear on Earth

Dividing the hours

Hours are divided into **60 minutes**. **Minutes** are then divided into **60 seconds**. This system dates from the ancient Babylonians, who chose the number 60 because it can be **divided exactly** by lots of different numbers: **2, 3, 4, 5, 6, 10, 12, 15, 20 and 30.**

Counting the years

As we add up the years, we do so in **multiples of 10**. 10 years are a **decade**. 100 years are a **century**, while 1,000 years are a **millennium**.

When talking about time on the scale of the history of the Universe, scientists often talk of **mya**, which stands for 'millions of years ago', and **bya**, which stands for billions of years ago.

Leap years

Most years are **365 days long**, but the time it takes for the Sun to return to the same place in the sky each year is actually 365.24 days. To make a correction, every four years an extra day is added to make a leap year. However, this makes an average of **365.25 days**, which is a little too long, so 3 times every 400 years, a leap year is missed off.

A year is a leap year if:
Either it is divisible by 400, or it is divisible by four, but not divisible by 100.

540 mya

First animals appear

250 mya

First dinosaurs appear

65 mya

Dinosaurs disappear

200,000 years ago

First humans appear

What are we measuring?

Measurements can give different answers depending on what you use to make the measurement and where you make it.

Losing weight

"Where are the scales?"

The weight of an object varies depending on where we are weighing it. The farther away from Earth you go, the weaker the force of gravity. This means you lose weight by climbing mountains, but only a little! At the top of Mount Everest, climbers weigh about 0.25 per cent less than they do at the sea level.

Walking on the Moon

The difference in weight is much more dramatic when you travel to the Moon. A human who weighs **100 kg on Earth** will weigh **just 17 kg** on the surface of the Moon. That's $1/6$th the weight. Because of the weaker gravity, astronauts on the Moon had to take care when walking around. If they tried to walk like we do on Earth, they would fly up into the air and fall over.

How long is the coastline of an island?

The length of a wiggly line will vary depending on the means of measurement you are using. If you measure the line with a ruler, the answer will be bigger the shorter the ruler you use, as you will be able to follow more of the wiggles.

Measuring the coastline of the island Great Britain using lines of **100 km** gives a length of

2,800 km.

With lines of **50 km**, it is **3,400 km**, **600 km** longer. If you walk the whole coast, using lines one pace (about 1 metre) long, it will be much longer still – around

18,000 km.

So how long, exactly, is the coastline of Great Britain?

It all depends on how you measure it.

A stiff tape measure can only measure objects in straight lines.

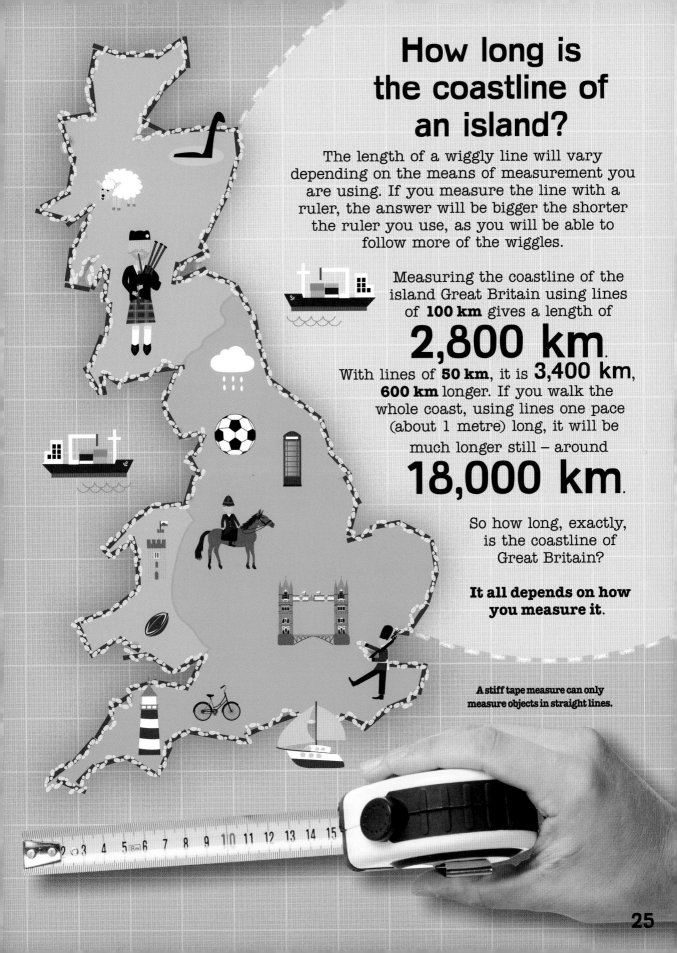

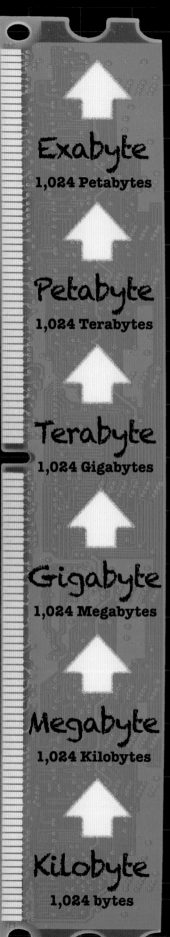

Exabyte
1,024 Petabytes

Petabyte
1,024 Terabytes

Terabyte
1,024 Gigabytes

Gigabyte
1,024 Megabytes

Megabyte
1,024 Kilobytes

Kilobyte
1,024 bytes

How fast is your computer?

The smallest unit in a computer memory is the bit. This can have one of two values: either 'on' or 'off' ('0' or '1'). Bits are arranged into groups of eight, called bytes. Individual pieces of information are stored on bytes, which form the 'words' of the memory. For example:

01101001 11011110

Each bit in a byte can take one of two values. This means that the total different values a byte can take is

$$2 \times 2 \times 2 \times 2 \times 2 \times 2 \times 2 \times 2 = 256$$

Computer memory, called the hard drive, has grown in size hugely since the earliest computers. Modern computers have enormous numbers of bytes in their memory.

1956	**1984**	**2012**	**2015**
The IBM 305 RAMAC had a memory of about 5 megabytes.	The first Apple Mac computer had a memory of 128 kilobytes.	The super computer Titan has a memory of 700 terabytes.	A modern smart phone has about 16 gigabytes of memory.

Hands on

The Chinese supercomputer **Tianhe-2** can perform 300 quadrillion operations in one second. That's 300,000,000,000,000,000 operations! Every human being on Earth, performing one calculation per second, would take more than a year to perform as many calculations as Tianhe-2 performs in a second.

Computer speed

With such huge memories, computers need to work very quickly. The processing speed of modern home computers is measured in gigahertz (GH).

1 gigahertz is equal to 1 billion operations per second.

"Hold on, wait a second!"

"A jiffy is quicker!"

A jiffy

Computers have internal clocks that they use to time their operations. One click on a computer's clock is called a 'jiffy'.

1 jiffy = about 10 ms (10 milliseconds) or 0.01 seconds

Quiz

50 million km

1 After the Moon, the brightest object in the night sky is the planet **Venus**. At its closest to **Earth**, Venus is about

50 million kilometres away.

If light takes **8 minutes** to reach us from the Sun, **how long does light take to reach us** from Venus?

2 **How many litres** of water would it take to half-fill a cube-shaped box with sides

20 cm long?

3 You see a bolt of lightning and count **9 seconds** before

hearing the thunder. **How far away** was the lightning?

4 a) Running at a steady speed of **25 m/s**,

how long would it take

a cheetah to complete a **100 m** race?

9 SECONDS

b) If a man running at

10 m/s starts

the race **level** with the cheetah, **how far behind** will the man be when the cheetah **crosses the line?**

5 How much **weight** have these weightlifters lifted? **Hint:** *look back at page 19 for the weights of the different colours. Don't forget the weights of the barbell and the collars.*

a) Barbell, collars, 2 red large, 2 green large, 2 blue small

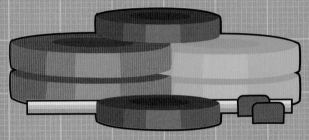

b) Barbell, collars, 4 yellow large

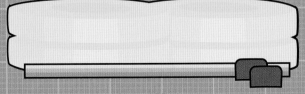

c) Barbell, collars, 2 blue large, 2 red small, 2 white small

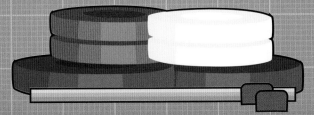

6 When he landed on the Moon, astronaut Neil Armstrong was wearing a space suit that weighed

82 kg on Earth.

Armstrong himself weighed **80 kg**. Remembering that the Moon has $\frac{1}{6}$ the gravity of Earth, how much did Armstrong in his spacesuit weigh on the Moon?

7 a) Convert these temperatures to degrees **Fahrenheit**:

a) **15°C**

b) **-5°C**

c) **100°C**

8 Convert these temperatures to degrees **Celsius**

a) **32°F**

b) **104°F**

c) **-40°F**

9 a) Venus is the hottest planet in the Solar System, with an average temperature at the surface of

735 Kelvin.

How much is this in °C (to the nearest whole degree)?

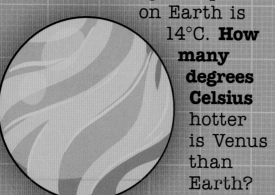

b) The average temperature on Earth is 14°C. **How many degrees Celsius** hotter is Venus than Earth?

F   C

120 — — 50

100 — — 40

80 — — 30

60 — — 20

— — 10

40 —

— — 0

20 —

— — -10

0 —

— — -20

-20 — — -30

-40 — — -40

10 Which of the following years is not a leap year?

a) **2000**

b) **2032**

c) **2100**

11 Your new computer has a processing speed of

2.8 gigahertz.

How many operations can it perform in **10 seconds?**

12 The 1984 Apple computer had

128 kilobytes

of memory. A certain new smart phone has **12.8 gigabytes** of memory. How many times more memory does the phone have than the Apple computer.

Hint: *first convert the phone's memory into kilobytes. (There are approximately 1 million kilobytes in a gigabyte. Use this value.)*

Glossary

Acceleration
A change in an object's velocity, caused by applying a force. Acceleration can change the object's speed, the direction in which it is moving, or both.

Byte
The basic unit in a computer's memory. One byte is made of eight bits, each of which can take the value 0 or 1. A byte can take 256 different values.

Gigahertz
A measure of frequency equal to 1 billion cycles per second.

Gravity
A force that pulls bodies with mass towards one another. The larger a body's mass, the greater its pull.

Imperial
A system of measurements that was standardised across the British Empire in the 19th century. Many of the measurements are related to the body, such as the inch, foot and yard.

Kelvin
A measure of temperature. 0 Kelvin (0 K), also known as absolute zero, is the minimum possible temperature. 0 K = -273.15°C

Leap year
A year that is 366 days long, one day longer than non-leap years. The extra day keeps years in step with Earth's orbit around the Sun.

Light year
A unit of length equal to the distance travelled by light in one year. Light travels at a speed of 299,792,458 metres per second, which means that in a year it travels 9.46 trillion km.

Mass
A measure of the amount of matter contained in an object.

Metric
A standard system of measurement that uses units in multiples of ten. Also called the International System of Measurement, it contains three main units: the metre, kilogram and litre.

Nanotechnology
Engineering that takes place at the nanoscale, which is between 1 and a few hundred nanometres (billionths of a metre). At this scale, machines are built using individual molecules as their moving parts.

Velocity
A measure of an object's movement. Velocity is the speed of motion in a particular direction. Any change in speed or direction changes an object's velocity.

Weight
A measure of the force of gravity pulling any object towards the centre of Earth. The weight of an object is roughly the same wherever it is on Earth.

Index

absolute zero 20
acceleration 16
acre 12
acre-foot 14
Alpha Centauri 9
Amazon Rainforest 13
Andromeda 9
Astronomical Unit (AI) 8
athletics track 7

bacteria 10
beard-second 11
bit 26
blue whale 18–19
body temperature 20
byte 26

Celsius 20–21
centimetre 6
cubic light year 15
cubit 4

DNA 10

Egypt 4
Einstein, Albert 17
Etruscan shrew 19
Everest, Mount 24

Fahrenheit 20
foot 5

gigahertz 27
gram 18
gravity 16, 24

hand 4, 5
hectare 12–13
Hipparcus 22
horse 4
hours 22
hydrogen atom 10

imperial system 5, 12
inch 4, 5

jiffy 27

Kelvin 20–21
kilogram 18–19
kilometre 6

league 7
leap year 23
light speed 17
light year 9
litre 14

MACS067-JD 9
metre 5, 6–7
metric system 5, 12, 14
micron 10
mile 6
Milky Way 9
millimetre 6
minute 23
month 22
Moon 21, 24

nanometre 10
nanotechnology 11

picometre 10
Planck length 11

satellite 16
second 23
Solar System 8
square metre 12
Sun 8, 21
sundial 22
swimming pool 15

TEU 14
thumb, rule of 4
Tianhe-2 27
tonne 19

weightlifting 19

yard 5
year 22, 23

Answers

5. a) 99 kg b) 85 kg c) 71 kg
6. Total weight on Earth = 162 kg.
162 ÷ 6 = 27 kg
7. a) 59°F b) 23°F c) 212°F
8. a) 0°C b) 40°C c) -40°C
9. a) 735 – 273 = 462°C
b) Venus is 448°C hotter than Earth
10. c) 2100 is not a leap year. It is divisible by 100, but not divisible by 400.
11. It performs 2.8 billion operations in one second, so in 10 seconds, it will perform 28 billion operations.
12. There are 1 million kilobytes in 1 gigabyte, so the phone has 12.8 million kilobytes of memory.
12.8 million ÷ 128 = 100,000

1. The Sun is 150 million km away. This is three times the distance of Venus, so the light from Venus takes $^8/_3$ minutes to reach us = 2 minutes 40 seconds
2. The volume of the box is 20 × 20 × 20 = 8,000 cm³ = 8 litres. To half-fill the box, you will need 4 litres of water.
3. 3 kilometres
4. a) It would take 4 seconds. b) After 4 seconds, the man will have covered 40 m, so he will be 60 metres behind.